DEFINE AND DIRECT

Build the life YOU want to live

Nick Gilbert

Contents

Prologue
Define and Direct 1

Chapter 1
Your Worst Enemy. 3

Chapter 2
Your Most Valuable Asset 8

Chapter 3
Simplification = Success 13

Chapter 4:
Self Negotiating = Self Sabotage. 18

Chapter 5
Hard 21

Chapter 6
Don't Worry About "Them" 24

Chapter 7
WHAT DO YOU REALLY WANT? 26

Chapter 8
Define and Direct 29

Chapter 9
Four Cornerstones 33

Chapter 10
Be Intentional 41

About the Author 44

Define and Direct

I wish I had a grand story to tell you about overcoming some catastrophic addiction, escaping a communist country, or fighting and surviving in a war - *but I don't.* The truth is, I am a normal dude who was born and raised in central Wyoming.

I was raised to work hard, respect people, and save money. I grew up in a blue-collar family and a *very* blue-collar state. I have struggled as most of you probably have, too: no money, relationship issues, drama, failed business, failed college, overweight, too much alcohol, workaholic attitude. . . You name the shit; we all go through it.

I am not a special person. Sure, I've helped some people work through some hard things, and I can relate to feeling stuck, feeling afraid, feeling angry, feeling depressed, feeling anxious, being broke, being broken, and struggling through messy relationships. I have been a teacher, coach, mentor, business owner, rodeo cowboy, "athlete," father, husband, failure, success, depressed, anxious, broke, well-off, confused, stuck, fat, skinny, leader, drunk. I lived a life of no direction. I have struggled and failed in ALL aspects of my life at one time or another. I have fought, and still fight, those battles. So, believe me when I say that I am not special. What separates me is that I keep going. Do I lose? *Yes. More often than not,* but I learn from those lessons and *I move forward.*

- I am not the wealthiest person on the planet, but I have built successful businesses.

- I am not the greatest husband on the planet, but after 15 years, our marriage is stronger than ever.

- I am not the greatest father on the planet, but I have worked hard to create kind and productive kids.

- I am not the fittest person on the planet, but I work hard to stay fit and healthy

The point: I am not perfect, and I have fucked up more than most. **The difference**: I have played the game over and over. I continue to play, and learn, and grow, and expand my life - personally, financially, and in my relationships.

My goal for this book is not to feed you full of guru and influencer bullshit. My goal is to show the reality of what has changed in my life to make me a better human. I am not blind to the fact that the shit I have gone through might be bigger than some of your shit, but some of you have gone through much bigger shit than I have. Regardless, we all go through things, and we all have some fucked up part of our lives. The difference is this: *some of us sit in our shit, and some of us scoop it and move on.* All of us have the ability to make that choice. I have witnessed rich kids turn into scum bags. I have witnessed poor kids grow up into wealthy adults. I have witnessed rich kids stay rich, and I have witnessed poor kids stay poor. Ultimately, it is a choice we GET to make.

Still, every single day, I watch people who are much smarter and more talented than me live a "normal" life. They go to work, go home, eat trash, watch TV, go to bed, and repeat the cycle. Does this sound familiar? If this is you, you are wasting a precious life. *You* had a 1 in 400 trillion chance of being born, and you are going through the motions. You are unhappy. You are waiting for retirement. You are waiting for the lottery. You are waiting for the raise. You are waiting for the right time. You are waiting for someone to save you. You are waiting for the cheat code. You are waiting. Waiting. Waiting. You are hoping everything in your life will play out the way it is supposed to. I already told you; I was that dude, and it is a daily battle for me to not slip back and be that dude again. However, I want to be the ONE who changes the trajectory of my family. I want my kids to dream. I want them to chase their goals. I want them to live a fulfilling life! So, if I expect that of them, then I must expect that of myself. It is very simple, but it is not easy. In fact, mostly it is inconvenient and hard. If you are breathing, you can still create purpose for yourself and for others.

If you find yourself waiting, chances are that *thing* you're waiting for is not going to happen. There is so much more for you to give to yourself, to your family, and to the world. My goal for you and for this book is that you can take at least ONE thing and implement it to direct your life in the direction you want it to go.

Chapter 1

Your Worst Enemy

"As a man thinketh in his heart so he is."

"Thought in the mind hath made us, what we are

by thought was wrought and built. If a man's mind

has evil thoughts, pain comes on him as comes

The wheel the ox behind......

If one endure

In purity of thought, joy follows him

As his own shadow—sure."

As a Man Thinketh by James Alenn

The average lifespan is 76-78 years. The average retirement age is 64-67 years. Assuming these numbers are accurate, you will have, on average, 11 - 12 years of life to do "whatever you want." Of course, this is assuming that you have put away enough money, the stock market doesn't crash, inflation stays in a place you can afford, and you are healthy. This is the model you have been pushed to believe as "normal." *There is really nothing normal about it.*

Most people wait until they are retired to start "checking off items on their bucket list." Newsflash: you might not make it to retirement. You might not wake up tomorrow. But, you do have a choice whether to buy into the narrative or *to create the life that you want to live.*

When we are young, we have the tendency to dream. We envision the life we were going to have when we grew up. We begin to grow and mature, and those dreams start to fade away. The question is: why? Why do we stop dreaming and imagining as we grow older? The answer: because it is not "normal." It does not fit the narrative. We have to forget those "childish dreams" and join the "real world." Before we know it, we are stuck in a job we hate and hanging around people who have accepted convenience and complacency. We begin to blame others, blame the world, blame society, blame our boss, blame the economy, blame everything and everyone - except for one aspect that really deserves the blame - YOU. The only person or thing that can truly control you is YOU.

Wherever you are in your life right now is 100% your fault.

The excuses in your mind are already arguing that statement.

> **You:** *But Nick, "I've had childhood trauma, abusive relationships, shitty parents, illnesses, bad experiences. . ."*

> **Me:** These experiences are an excuse to why you are not where you want to be.

Sure, maybe there is some validity to these excuses, but bad things happen to ALL OF US - bad things that are out of our control. But for every bad experience, there are people who have triumphed and are very, very successful. There are people who have had it far worse than *you*. Those people figured out a way to WIN and be productive in their lives.

Every single person has a story. Every single person has good and bad days. We all go through the shit. But you have to choose to accept it or rise above it. It is a decision you have to make to be great, or to stay in the same spot and live the same life *day after day after day* until you die. Ultimately, success and change are found in those experiences that we never want to relive. The experiences we have that cause discomfort, agony, and defeat are where true growth can happen. This is where we can make the decision to move forward and grow.

Your mindset will determine WHERE you go and how FAR you go. You've heard the saying by Henry Ford: "Whether you think you can, or you think you can't--you're right." Henry Ford is spot on, so stop downgrading your capabilities. Being GREAT is a CHOICE. Being BROKEN is a CHOICE. The choices you have made up to this point explain why you are where you are. Feeling stuck? That is your CHOICE. Waiting for the right time? That is your CHOICE. Your mind and body will take you where you want to go *if you allow it.* You are not entitled to success and you do not deserve it until you earn it, but you must take care of the person in the mirror to make your goals and dreams become reality.

But you don't have to be in this alone.

If you do not have coaches or mentors, you should find some. All high achievers have surrounded themselves with great people to help them succeed. Kobe Bryant and Michael Jordan had Tim Grover. Kobe Bryant and Michael Jordan are arguably the greatest to ever play the game of basketball, yet they hired the best trainer to help them be better. They acknowledged a need to improve and made a CHOICE to seek guidance to improve their craft. *It is not a coincidence.*

However, when you hire a coach, understand they are not there to "save you." A coach's job is to influence and push you to new levels, but ultimately **YOU** have to put in the **WORK**. Read all the books you want. Follow all the successful people you want. Listen to all the self-improvement podcasts you want. Hire all the coaches you want. Nothing will EVER happen until **YOU TAKE ACTION**. *You* must take the steps to be better. *You* must start the process. *You* must understand that sometimes the actions you take are going to be wrong, but you must adapt, pivot, and solve the problem. No matter what anyone says, there will be setbacks on your journey. YOU must be willing to accept that and keep moving forward. You cannot fixate on past mistakes, and you cannot predict the future. You have to control the controllables: time, emotions, fitness, health, money, and relationships.

What if I fail?

This is not an if, but a when. When you fail, change your mindset. Do not consider it a failure; it is a lesson. How would you have known any different if you had never tried? Failure and defeat are the greatest teachers. This is where growth happens. You must learn to embrace it, harness it, and get better. Whatever it is you are going to do, you will fail at some point. It might be a large failure or a small failure, but bad things are going to happen, and mistakes are going to be made. Will you wallow in self-doubt, or will you own the mistake and make the necessary corrections?

Your mindset is a choice you make from the moment you wake up every day. If you woke up this morning, you have already won. There are a bunch of people who have not woken up from last night. Their time on this earth is *done*. If you are reading this, you are ALIVE. What are you going to do with it? You get another opportunity in this life! You have a choice to waste it or take advantage of the opportunity. You have been awarded a gift. Be grateful you have been given another day; do not waste it.

The mindset of fear, scarcity, and lack of belief is a learned behavior. When you were learning to walk, you were not afraid or disbelieving. Everyone around you was encouraging you, clapping for you, and filming you. Your success made them happy, and believe it or not, made your baby brain feel accomplished and loved. You had the approval of others to continue walking and growing. Unfortunately, as we grow up, this mindset is eventually replaced with an idea of how you "should" be living. Stop daydreaming and face reality. You don't believe me? Think back to your school days. What happened when you got good grades vs. poor grades? You were taught to sit in that desk, pay attention, raise your hand, behave, and if you did all this, you would be able to live a "normal" life. If you did not, you were told you would be "flipping Whoppers." You would be a failure according to societal norms.

This could not be further from the truth. Truthfully, the American Education System thrives on compliance. If you do as you are told, you will be rewarded. However, that is a standard "they" set for you, and not the standard *you should be setting for yourself*. We buy into it because that is how we were *trained* to think. Yet, you have the ability to change the entire narrative, but most will not. Most of us will continue through the motions of life because *change is inconvenient and difficult*. We will spend our days relying on others, gossiping, and "keeping up with the Joneses." If we change or pursue something different, we are afraid of ridicule or judgment from others.

Fun Fact: We are all going to die one day.

And most of us will be forgotten by everyone except our immediate family. As generations move forward, our memory will get pushed further behind. So, why do we care so much? *You must get out of your own way.* Stop overthinking. Stop believing the narrative that only certain people can have _____ (fill in the blank). Stop discounting your abilities. Stop waiting for things to happen. You cannot predict the future, and you cannot relive the past. All you can control is what is happening right now, *today.* You have the opportunity every day to make a change to better your life and your environment. It will be hard. There will be challenges, but *YOU* must decide what is worth fighting for.

Will you live a life you want to live, by your own rules, or will you let other factors decide it for you? Every day that you wake up, you get to make a choice. You get to choose your emotions, your perspective, your mindset, the food you eat, the drinks you drink, the workout you do, the shows you watch, and the podcasts you listen to. Only YOU can control those factors. Do NOT blame your circumstances. CHANGE THEM!

Chapter 2

Your Most Valuable Asset

If you lose money, you can make it back. If you lose time, it is gone forever.

Have you ever experienced scrolling through social media, your local newspaper, or news feed when you land on the obituary section? You notice a familiar face and your heart sinks a little bit. Even if you have not seen or spoken to that person for years, it still has an impact on you. You read the obituary, and then maybe you send your condolences, but then you move on with your life.

One day, that obituary will be yours. It's no secret: you will not be on this planet forever. One day, you will leave your home and never return. You do not know when that day will be, but one thing is for sure: your time is coming. Your hourglass will eventually empty, and your most valuable asset will be gone. *Time* is the only asset that you cannot get back. It is the only asset that can define your entire life. We all have the same 24 hours in a day. How we CHOOSE to use that time is the separator. We choose to make excuses for our time. We CHOOSE to use our time for meaningless work. We CHOOSE to use our time to gossip. We CHOOSE to use our time for drama. We CHOOSE to use our time to feed addictions.

What you do with your time on this planet is your choice. If you CHOOSE to use it to be fat...Cool. If you choose to use it to be a drunk...neat. If you CHOOSE to use it to be the ONE who changes your family dynamic.....HELL YEAH!

How much time do you waste on meaningless "things" each day? As we grow older, we look back and wonder, "Where did the years go?" We simply proceed through the motions of life until we realize we are 40, 50, 60, 70, 80 years old if we are lucky. But, even if you are 40, you still have a shit load of life left in front of you to do BIG things. It all comes down to how you choose to navigate your time. However, until you can manage your time, you have no control over your life.

Of course, that is easier said than done. The world today is full of distractions. The average person is focused for only three to four hours per day. What's happening during the other 20-21 hours? Most are sleeping or engaging in unproductive activities. Our daily lives are full of STUFF. Most of the "STUFF" we occupy our minds with are actually distractions - **distractions from productivity.**

How much time do you waste on distractions each day?

Don't know? Don't care? Imagine if you could eliminate distractions and get back *just one focused hour per day.* That is 365 hours a year of focused, meaningful, and purposeful work. Imagine the possibilities just by gaining back that *one hour.* Why is it that some people can get so much more done than others in a day? Is it because they are smarter? Do they work Harder?

The answer is simple.

They learn to eliminate distractions and focus on the tasks in front of them. They are *present in the moment.* **If it does not add value. They do not spend their time on it.** The distractions go away, and they are focused and efficient. It is not a natural behavior, but something that is learned and practiced, and mastered over time. High achieving people can take tasks that take eight hours and condense them into three or four. This leaves nearly three or four more hours to build bigger or "go play."

We all have that ability, but most of us will not take the time to understand how much time we waste in a day, week, or year. Because I believe in practicing what I preach, I decided to analyze how much time I wasted on a given day. To do this, you must determine what is **valued production** and what is a **distraction**, but if it is not adding value to your life, it is a distraction. If you are in the middle of work, and your bestie calls to tell you about how drunk he got last night = distraction.

That shit is not productive, nor is it adding value to your life. You do not have to answer every call, text, or email on the spot. If you are that person, shut it off and focus on the task at hand. Minimizing those distractions will lead to more efficient and meaningful work. When you do this activity and if you are honest with yourself, you will find that you are wasting hours in a day, or you will find that many of the tasks you are working on are not really moving your life or career forward.

A few examples:

Valued Production	Distraction
+ Work	− Gossip (BIGGEST ONE)
+ Exercise	− Social Media (unless used for marketing)
+ Personal Development	
+ Books (smut is not valuable)	− Meaningless conversation
+ Business Growth	− Employees having too much access to you
+ Meaningful meetings (efficient)	
+ Business calls	− Shitty lunch (fast food garbage)
+ Date Night	− Drama
+ Nutrition	− Family (When just calling to BS)
+ Meditation	− Email/Text notifications
+ Time with kids	
+ Investments	

24 Time Audit: Track 24 hours of your day. It can start whenever you want just make sure it is 24 hours.

1. In your phone notes or on a piece of paper, write down the word **Distractions** at the top.

2. Throughout 24 hours, write down when you are distracted. A distraction in this case is taking away from the things that serve or add value to you. Basically, your production.

    Example: If you are in the middle of writing up a huge proposal and Karen calls to gossip about her husband, *that would be a distraction.*

3. Each time you are distracted, write down the amount of time you were distracted for.

    Note: each time you are interrupted or distracted add a minimum of 1 minute - even if it was 10 seconds - because the amount of time it takes to refocus will add up to about a minute.

4. Be honest- this activity does not work if you are not being truthful with yourself.

When I created this time audit for myself, I found that I wasted nearly 3.5 hours everyday on meaningless tasks. When I corrected those behaviors, my stress levels went down, production went up, business grew, my health improved, and my ability to be more flexible with my free time increased. Through practice, and trial and error, I have learned to maximize my time each day. I have learned that I can accomplish so much more if I am intentional with how I use my time.

Things I found that occupied way too much of my time:

- Social Media scrolling
- "Water cooler" talk
- Texts
- Monitoring and answering every email
- Phone calls
- Employees
- Customers
- Meetings with no purpose
- Gossip

In business and government, so much time is wasted on meetings. As a leader, you must decide which meetings are essential and which meetings are worthless. Do not meet "just to meet" because that is how "it has always been done." In my experience, most meetings are 70% a waste of time and 30% productive. Chances are you can probably get through the important stuff in a meeting within 30 minutes or less, but you must *cut the shit*, get laser focused on the objective, and get it done!

What does this look like in practice? Create time where you can. For example, you might have "office hours" where you cut yourself off from EVERYTHING for a two hour period. Or, you might get up earlier and stay up later than the rest of the world to focus on your work.

Instead of stopping by the employee lounge every time you go to the restroom, you take a different route to avoid the distractions.

Turn your phone off, log out of your apps, close your email, turn off the office phone. You can correct the behaviors and create more meaningful time for yourself. *Time is a precious commodity.* You cannot make more of it, but you can make the most of it. Once it is gone, it is gone. Stop wasting it.

FOMO? (Fear Of Missing Out)

Right now, you are thinking the above is impossible because you might *miss out* on something important. Nothing is as important as the task you are focused on at the time. The task that is helping you accomplish your goals and targets. If there is something more import-ant, you need to refocus your priorities. It takes recognizing and ad-mitting that you are spending too much time on the wrong things, and then correcting the action. You must be disciplined enough to stick with your time commitments and schedules.

In my life, I've discovered that I need to wake up around 4:00 AM each weekday. Why? Because, for me, mornings are peaceful, and I can get a lot of meaningful work done. I do my best work in the morning. If I am not up before the sunrise, I feel like I am already behind, so I wake up early and get after it. That is how I CHOOSE to use my time.

Ultimately, get out of bed when you want. Whether it is 4:00 AM or 4:00 PM, it doesn't really matter. What matters is what you do with the time you are awake. At first, when you learn to control your time, it will feel weird because the chaos in your life will dwindle. You will feel more in control, but you might feel a little "stir crazy" because you have all your important shit done and now you have free time. Take that "free time" and use it for yourself. Invest your time in getting to the next level of your life or business opportunity.

The point: stop dealing with people and activities that are a waste of time and a waste of production. Sure, sometimes sitting down and watching TV or doing something mindless is okay, but that should take place AFTER the work is done. YOU make the choice to make your time on this planet purposeful.[1]

---

1 **Two books I recommend for time management:**
AMRAP Mentality by Jason Khalipa
The One Thing by Gary Keller and Jay Papason

Chapter 3

Simplification = Success

Indecision and complexity are the creators of chaos.

I used to own a lawn and landscape business. It was small, but we started out by simply mowing lawns. We were building and growing. I had employees. My company was good at mowing lawns. We were so good that people wanted us to start taking on other projects for them. Power raking (dethatching), aerating, clean-ups. . .so we started to do that. It turns out, we were pretty good at that, too. Then customers wanted us to start doing landscape projects: plant trees, install sod, rocks, sprinklers, pavers etc. So naturally, we expanded. We were certainly busy with the extra workload, but I did not know how to do a lot of it, and things became chaotic. I had to research and experiment to find the answers. I ended up outsourcing a fair amount of our work, and it cost me both money and headaches. My team was good at LAWN CARE, but I chose to expand into the other "stuff." We made it work, grew the company, and sold the whole thing.

Success? Sort of. But the moral of the story is that I made the company too complex. We were good at LAWN CARE, but mediocre at the rest. Tending to all the other "stuff" took away from what we were really good at. If I were to do it over again, I would stick to what we did best and most efficiently: Lawn Care. In retrospect, I could have doubled my lawn care client list rather than jumping into all the different services, making more money with far less headache.

Those lessons carried over to my sign shop. At the beginning, we were using countless products for different applications, so I could give people a better price. The problem was I only used some products sparingly, so I was stuck with inventory that we would have to throw out. I quickly made the decision to find the best product that would fit most of our customers' needs. We simplified our product line, and it has decreased the headaches and increased our profits. Our business has grown, our profits are up, and all it took was to make a decision to simplify our product.

Simple.

If you are really good at donuts and coffee, why would you expand and start to sell hamburgers and tacos? You are good at DONUTS AND COFFEE. Sell more of those. *Simple.* Do you see Crumble Cookies selling cheese burgers? No, they sell the best fucking cookies on the planet all over the country. *Simple.*

Simplify your systems to increase effectiveness. I have witnessed and participated in some complicated systems - systems that I never really understood. Systems that took 800 steps to get to the result. Most of the time, we could have eliminated even half of the steps and arrived at the result quicker. If you find yourself spending more time trying to figure things out rather than moving on actionable items, chances are your systems are too complicated and need to be simplified. Do you want to guarantee a stressful team environment? Then create complicated systems that are difficult to navigate. Do you want a productive and happy team? Then simplify the process. Make things as clear and concise as humanly possible. So, why do we feel like we need to add all these "things" to our stores and lives? Mostly because we are people pleasers. If we have more products, we will reach more people, right?. Unfortunately, it is really hard to be REALLY good at multiple things. You might draw in a large crowd with many different interests, but can you offer a quality product and experience for ALL of them? Doubtful. By trying to please everyone, you are actually causing yourself more stress and anxiety and you will please no one. Understand that you and your product(s) *are not for everyone.* SIMPLIFY. Offer your best product to the people who will buy it and appreciate it. Then find more of those people and do more of that thing you are good at and is working.

Simplicity is the same for all facets of our lives.

Simplify Nutrition.

Are you struggling with nutrition? Nutrition is one of the most complex aspects on the planet because we make it that way. There are so many fad diet plans out there that people continue to buy. It is hard to determine which is right for you. There is so much information about what you should do to improve your nutrition: Keto, Gluten Free, fasting, etc. People get frustrated because they do not see the results immediately, so they go back to their old ways of eating and drinking whatever makes them feel good. People try something and it doesn't work, so they give up and just stay fat. I am no nutrition expert, but I found a simple way to lose weight and "get shredded."

I eliminated 3 things from my diet:

- Anything with processed or added sugar or high fructose corn syrup

- Processed meats

- Alcohol

Notice that I did not say anything about counting calories or messing with macros and micros. I did not say anything about eating simple versus complex carbs, gluten free, or any other fad diet. No meal prepping. In my opinion, these are complicated and when they don't work, people give up.

However, eliminating these three things will eliminate a whole mess of foods that are shitty for you and it is *simple.* If you pick it up and it says added sugar, put it down. Processed meat...just say no. Beer, Whiskey.....no thanks. *Simple shit.* I did not over complicate it, reinvent the wheel, or take weight loss supplements. I am a *simple* person. I watch people at the gym drink pre-workouts, drink a mix during workouts, and then have post- workout shakes. Then go home and weigh their food. Who has time for all that? If that works for you, okay! But, if you are spending more than ten minutes a day preparing your nutrition, that shit is *too complicated* ,and you are overthinking. You are wasting valuable time and resources. Remember that thing about time: you don't get it back.

Simplify Fitness.

Are you struggling with fitness? One of the busiest and most complicated places is a large gym. You walk in, look to the right, and there are the Crossfitters. They are moving fast from exercise to exercise, yelling, grunting, and pouring sweat all over the gym floor. Then you look around the corner and there are the people pulling on all different colors of bands with their legs, arms, and moving in all sorts of weird directions. Then you spin a 180 and there are machines and people moving the weights on the machines. As you walk past them, you notice the dumbbells, the benches, and barbells, and some jacked men and women yelling at each other to lift more! You think you might be in the wrong part of the gym, so you turn back to the cardio section with all the ellipticals, treadmills, stair steppers and bikes. Some people are casually walking or pedaling. A few folks are taking their time on the stair stepper, climbing the reciprocating mountain of steps. To the left, there is the dude sprinting as fast as he can on the treadmill and the lady next to him on the elliptical violently throwing her arms and legs to make the machine appear like it could catch fire due to friction. You become lost because of the overwhelming amount of machines and exercises people are doing. You are not sure what is right and what is wrong. "What should I do?" you ask yourself. Then you stand there looking like a dummy trying to figure it out.

First of all, go to the gym with a plan. What is the goal you have in mind for yourself and what is it going to take to get there? If you want to look like Arnold Schwarzenegger and bench 300, hit the heavy weights. If you want to be able to run a marathon, hit the treadmill. You must have an objective of what you want to do with your body and what you want it to look like. If you are new to the gym environment, I would suggest hiring a trainer or joining a class. *Simple.* They do all the programming for you. All you have to do is show up and move your body like they tell you to. No sense in trying to reinvent the wheel.

We take the most simplistic things and turn them into arduous nightmares that lead us down a road of anxiety and stress. We over-analyze and think we need "all the things" to make something work. We need the "things" to make our life work. We need the "things" to make our business work. If we don't have "x," then "y," will happen. If "y" happens, we are doomed. We predict the problems before the problems occur, and then we freeze up and don't know where to go or where to turn. But, nothing has even happened yet. We have created "complex chaos" in our minds.

Paralysis by Analysis.

Paralysis by Analysis is when you are in a state of "What if...." Should I...." " I could have...." Maybe I should...." How many ideas, dreams, or goals have you talked yourself out of by overthinking? You over-analyze a decision that nine times out of ten has a simple answer, but you just have to weigh all the "options." Chances are, most of your "options" are hypothetical and will not happen anyways. So, simplify the process, make a decision, and take action.. As long as it is not life and death, everything is fixable. Whether wrong or right, you made the decision and now you have to *act on that decision.*

Nobody has a crystal ball predicting the future. Your decision could lead you to a pot of gold or a swamp full of alligators. You don't know until you make the decision and move forward. The more you sit, think, and stew over it, the more complicated it tends to become. We often spend so much time weighing out the pros and the cons that we delay the ACTION, or in some cases, we NEVER perform the action. Simplify your decision-making and ask yourself YES or NO questions:

- Does it serve me?
- Does it serve my cause?
- Will I grow and learn?
- Will it help me or someone else?
- Will it make me and others better?
- Is it purposeful?

These are just a few examples, but the more black and white you make the answers, the easier it is to answer the question and take action. We tend to debate because we do not have a simple plan or strategy in place; we do not have a simple target. What would be a simple target? *I am going to lose "x" pounds.* Now, when you start to negotiate with yourself about eating that twinkie or skipping that workout, you have the simple answer. The answer is "no," because now you have a purposeful target of losing weight. If you want to decrease stress and live a more joyful life, simplify everything you can. Make a decision and stick with it. Stop overthinking. Take action and make adjustments. Don't predict the problems, but have the ability to solve them as they come.

Chapter 4

Self Negotiating = Self Sabotage.

After seven years, I stepped into my principal's office and quit my job as an educator. It was about three years past due. For three years, I was miserable and it carried over into my marriage and my relationship with my kids. Other relationships began to suffer because of the anger and burden I carried with me each day. I spent three years negotiating with myself about quitting.

"I don't want to be labeled a quitter."

"I don't want to let my colleagues down."

"I don't want to let my students and athletes down."

"I don't want to put anyone in a bad spot."

"We need insurance."

"We need retirement."

"This is a 'secure' job."

"Am I just being soft?"

"My colleagues have toughed it out for years. I should be able to."

"How will we make ends meet in our family?"

During my self-negotiation, I was not helping anyone. I was not helping my colleagues, my students, my family, myself: NO ONE. I became of no value to anyone around me. I felt stuck and I actually believe that I pushed many people away because I was difficult to be around. I was negative. I was, simply put, an asshole. Had I made the decision to leave when I initially felt the urge, I would have gained three years of progress and growth, but instead, I sat in a pool of negativity and let it fester.

I could not bring myself to make the decision, but when I finally made the decision, a new world opened up to me. My thinking became more clear. I was able to focus on my future in peace. The burden of the decision was gone, and I could finally *scoop up my shit and move on*.

I spent three years trying to make this very simple decision, and I spent three years negotiating with myself. Looking back, I realized that I made this decision a much bigger deal than it really needed to be. Changing a career can be a risk, but you have to realize that with risk comes reward. The only regret I have is how long it took me to take the leap.

Many of you are in the same boat. You feel stuck. You feel empty. You feel burdened. When you enter this place of emotions, it makes decisions that much more difficult. The longer you negotiate, the more anxiety and angst you feel. *Your self-negotiations are sabotaging your progress.* When you spend more time debating rather than taking action, you become "stuck." You question yourself and your abilities. You get into your own head and start overthinking, or if you are like most people, you automatically jump to all of the things that "could" go wrong and negotiate yourself out of what could be a life changing decision.

Of course, you are trying to predict the future and decide what is "best." However, you must realize that every decision has a consequence. It does not matter how good or bad the decision is. Naturally, we debate which consequence might have the least negative impact on our lives. Aside from a life or death decision, you can not predict what is going to come of your decision at that time. Once the decision is made, you must stick with it. You must move forward. Accept the consequences. Adapt and move on. Living in the depth of past decisions will only hinder us from moving forward. Bad shit is going to happen, and even the best decisions come with trials.

So, try to switch your thinking: make a list of all the **positives** that could come of the decision you are stuck on making. Then ask yourself, **"What happens if I don't….?"** It is easy to list all the bad things that could arise, but rarely do we sit down and list the positives that could come from a simple decision. As long as you are breathing, everything is fixable.

Self Negotiation = Lack of Target

When you do not truly know what you want, creating a target makes decision making *simple*. When you establish a target and a question arises, the answer becomes easy.

- Is what I am doing, getting me to where I want to go? YES or NO?

- If I eat this, is it going to help my weight loss goal? YES or NO?

- I want to be a millionaire. Is whatI am doing going to get me closer? YES or NO?

When you have a clear direction, the decision-making process becomes easier. The negotiations go away. When you do not want to do something, but you know it will get you to your goals, the negotiation stops. So, the real question to ask yourself is: "What do you want?" Then, figure out what it is going to take to get there. If what you are doing is not getting you to your "want," you have to ask yourself, "Why am I doing it?"

So, do you want to slow your progress? Do you want to delay your growth? Keep negotiating with yourself. Keep pushing everything off until tomorrow. One of our largest hindrances is the negotiation we have within our own heads. Similar to the time audit, take 24 hours and count how many times you negotiate yourself out of ideas and decisions that might change your life forever.

Chapter 5

Hard

"When your mind and body are starting to tire and you feel like giving up, you're only at 40% of what you are truly capable of achieving."

- David Goggins

With the conveniences of our modern society, everything has become easily achievable. The devices in our hands have the capability to do almost anything we want with a click of a button. We can order food and have it delivered. We can buy clothes and have them delivered. We can use AI to help us complete tasks. These conveniences are both a blessing and a curse. They bless us with the ability to grow and expand our lives quicker than ever with more information at our fingertips than ever before. In fact, many of our problems can be solved by watching a 5 minute YouTube video. Life has become extremely convenient. "The curse", conveniences have also created a society of impatient and "soft" people.

When I say "soft," I mean that we are fatter than we have ever been. We do not handle adversity well. If we cannot solve the problem with the push of a button, we quit. Many of our jobs and education require us to sit and stare at a screen all day, and in reality, very few are willing to get out of their comfort zone, brave the elements, and do what needs to be done to find success and fulfillment. We have become robots in a system.

Most people are not willing to push themselves outside of their comfort zones and therefore they stay the same for their entire lives. Doing things that are scary and difficult, regardless of the result, will create a resiliency in you. America's biggest phobia is PUBLIC SPEAKING. It is scary and uncomfortable to speak in front of people; however, the more you do it, the easier it gets.

As a result, we must intentionally create difficult and hard situations. This seems strange and goes against the norm of what society tells us, but in order for us to grow and evolve as humans and a society, we must be able to handle difficult situations and difficult tasks *while keeping our emotions in check.* Tasks that push us out of our comfort zones also teach us to handle our emotions. We all have a "personal threshold" and when we meet that threshold, we tend to stop because that is our "breaking point." When you train yourself to get past that threshold, a whole new world opens to you. You become more confident, less emotional, more rational,, and you are able to make better decisions.

It is important to note that pushing out of your comfort zone is different for everybody. What might be hard for me, might be easy for you, and vice versa. If you gave me the choice to call 100 people and sell them a product, or to run a 52 mile ultra marathon, I would pick the ultra-marathon 100% of the time. Calling and selling is hard for me; it is unnatural because I actually HATE to sell to people. Yet, if you ask the next guy, he will tell you something different. Hard looks different for everyone. Whatever your "hard" is, approach it head on and learn to defeat it. I powered through the sales calls. I made it a priority to embrace the suck and the result was that I created a 7-figure company.

Working out is another important aspect in life that can be extremely difficult for people. I used to be nearly 220 pounds. Going to the gym was hard for me. I still don't like going to the gym, but I do it over and over and over because I know that I need to get past my comfort threshold. Most of my mornings consist of a cardio walk, run, or stadium stairs. Ultimately, running is not fun for me. I am slow and the first couple of miles always hurt. But, I learned that the more I push myself in fitness; the more I push myself in other areas of my life. I believe there is a direct correlation to having a fit mind and body, and excelling at business, relationships, careers, and life.

So, the more we push ourselves into hard situations, the more "gritty" we become. We are able to handle difficult situations with more poise, we solve problems, we take action, we build, we chase our dreams, we stop feeling stuck, and we eliminate emotional decisions. Emotions will never go away, but making sound decisions during high times and low times is critical to success.

How do you do this in practice? First, you have to understand that mastering the hard times is a process. If it is hard to run a mile, go run a mile - no matter how fast or slow. Then, master that mile. Improve your pace. Then run two miles, work to four miles, then work to eight. What was once hard now becomes easy and routine. Once it becomes routine, it is time to look for the next challenge. Of course, it is hard to continue to do things when the excitement runs out and becomes harder. We start to make excuses and find different avenues to make us feel good. This is a MISTAKE. The people that consistently crush it, keep showing up and making gains despite their motivation to do so.

Consider this: when you start a job or career, you may see a spike in your income quickly. Maybe, you were promoted quickly. You have passed the people you started with. You are excited and driven as you approach the top. Now you are working next to people who have climbed the ladder like you have. The competition gets stiffer for the next promotion. Now that you have higher level people competing against you, the entire game changes. It gets harder. Most people settle and are willing to accept their B level position because it gets too hard and inconvenient to compete against the A players. *Do not settle.*

"It is better to be a warrior in a garden than a gardener in a war."

– Sun Tzu

I know what you are thinking. Why would I put myself in hard situations if I don't have to?

My question is: Why wouldn't you? Are you prepared for when the family wealth runs dry? Are you going to be the one responsible for ruining a family legacy because you couldn't handle difficult obstacles? If everything was taken from you tomorrow, could you create it all again? Even Better? If someone entered your home to harm your family, would you have the ability to defend it? I can almost guarantee that you will not react as you think you will.

The world has many, many gardeners who think they are ready for war, but they have lived easy and simple lives. They have never lived through or created REAL adversity. Don't be a "gardener".

Chapter 6

Don't Worry About "Them"

Don't compare your beginning to someone else's middle, or your middle to someone else's end. Don't compare the start of your second quarter to someone else's third quarter.

-Tim Hiller

Want to stay stuck in your life? Compare yourself to others all day, every day.

When you are comparing yourself to others, you are stealing time from yourself. Time you should be focusing on you and your own shit. Why are you worried about them? If they have something you want, figure out how they did it. Meet with them, study them, but remember you are still you, and they are them.

You have different characteristics than any other human on the planet. It is easy to get caught up in, "I wish I had those skills", or "I wish I could sell like them." However, those skills are developed. Sure, some people are born with natural abilities, but sharpening and building your skills takes time, patience and hard work.

The people on social media or in society screaming, "look at me" with their swag and bling may not be as well off as you think. Movies, and social media have created a façade of what a "good life" looks like. They appear happy and successful and we crave it for ourselves. We want to feel the way they appear, but when we look at ourselves and our lives and realize we don't have that life, we feel inferior.

You do not know what is TRULY going on in their world and you cannot control what is going on in their world. If they drive a nicer car, good for them! If they have a nicer house, awesome!

How does that serve YOU? It doesn't. You can have what they have, but you cannot have it with a victim mentality and thinking about what they have and you don't. The focus has to be on YOU, not them. Focus on *your things*. Your dreams. Your life. Let them live theirs.

Comparing yourself to yourself is the ultimate recipe for growth and change.

Ask yourself these questions:

- How does the person today compare to the person yesterday?
- Is that person better or worse?

Your life should be about creating the best possible self you can and then sharing it with the world. When you are making changes and gains in your life, you will be judged. You may also look at others and feel like you are not making the same gains. Everyone is fighting a daily battle, and you have to determine: Am I better today than I was yesterday?

Don't expect anyone to pat you on the back when you are doing well. It will most likely be the exact opposite. Winning comes from battles you win daily with yourself - the demons and doubt that you slay each day, and the struggles you overcome. That is where confidence is built. That is where true growth is made.

As you grow personally, the world around you will change. Friends will change. Bank accounts will grow. You will look better and feel better. Winning the daily battle with yourself is so much more powerful than trying to win the battle against others. Win one day. Then the next, and then the next day after that. Go to bed at night KNOWING that YOU won the day.

Chapter 7

WHAT DO YOU REALLY WANT?

In the movie, *The Notebook* the character, Noah, played by Ryan Gosling, and Allie, played by Rachel McAdams, create what I believe is one of the most memorable scenes in the movie. It is not only a brilliant scene, but it is a reality in most of our lives.

Noah: *Would you do something for me, please. Just picture your life for me. 30 years from now, 40 years from now, what does it look like? If it's with that guy, go, go! I lost you once, I think I can do it again, if I thought it's what you really wanted. But don't you take the easy way out.*

Allie: What easy way? There is no easy way. No matter what I do, somebody gets hurt!

Noah: Would you stop thinking about what everyone wants! Stop thinking about what I want, what he wants, what your parents want. **What do you want? What do you want?**

Allie: It's not that simple.

Noah: What do you want? Damn it, what do you want?

For nearly 20 years, this scene has stuck with me. Not only is it a great love story, but it is also reality. In reality, most of us have no idea what we truly want. Part of the problem is that we have so many choices, so it is hard to narrow down what we want. So what should we do? The answer is to test as many things as possible to figure out what lights a fire inside your soul.

Certainly, many of us have an *idea* of what we want, but how detailed are you with those wants?

- Do you want to be rich? How rich? What does that actually look like?

- Do you want kids? How many? Why that number?

- Do you want to own a house? Where? How big? What color?

- Do you want nice cars? What kind?

- Do you want to own land? What kind? Where?
- Do you want peace? So, you want to be a monk? What does peace really mean?
- Do you want to live a purposeful life? What is your purpose?

  Ultimately, *what do you want?*

This is a very simple question that many cannot answer decisively. If I approached you on the street and asked you this question randomly, could you answer it directly and with confidence?

Could you explain to me *in detail* what it is that you want? Or would I get the same vague answers that most people give - "I want to make money" or "I want a nice house." What do those answers even mean?

Your want has to be detailed and visualized in your mind. It has to be so detailed that you could ask an artist to paint the exact picture you have in your mind. You have to get very clear and focused on what it is you want your life to look like.

So, what is stopping you from getting what you want in your life? What is stopping you from pursuing what you want? Are you willing to make sacrifices to get what you want?

Once again, it will not be easy. Discipline and consistency are hard, but having discipline and being consistent is what you must do to get what you want in your life. Stop worrying about what THEY want and what they think you need; become insanely focused on what you want. YOU are what matters.

In fact, your wants do not have to align with what society thinks you should want. We all want to be successful, but what does that actually mean to you? To me, that is living the life *I want to live.* I have met wealthy people that are miserable, and I have met poor people that are extremely happy. We are often sold on the idea that to be happy, we need to have wealth and abundance. However, while I think money makes our lives easier and more manageable by adding short term peace to our lives, wealth does not lead to ultimate happiness.

Many people are happy with what they have and where they are in life. They have everything they want. It is easy to look at wealth and THINGS and make the assumption that those are the happiest people on the planet, but the reality is: **PEOPLE WHO ARE LIVING THE LIFE THEY WANT TO LIVE ARE THE HAPPIEST.** There is absolutely nothing wrong with owning a bad ass car, massive home, 200 pairs of Nikes, fancy watches, and nice clothes. If this is the lifestyle you WANT, that is great for you.

There is another group of people who know exactly what they want, BUT they make every excuse not to get it. This is often because they have not developed a solid plan to achieve what it is they want. They let the distractions of life and society get in the way. The author of this book is guilty, and you probably are, too.

So how do you move past the distractions? Imagine someone giving you a key to a treasure and they point and say, "This chest is over there." "Over there" could be thousands of miles away or two miles away. Chances are, you will spend your life trying to find it and figure it out. You will most likely die trying to find it, or give up. Now, if they gave you the coordinates to the chest, you could quickly make your way to the chest because you have a TARGET and a plan to get there.

When you determine what it is you want in life, the path will not always be easy. It will likely be littered with roadblocks. However, you will have purpose and direction. You will be equipped to move in the direction you want to take. Ultimately, we are all capable, but you must take the first step in the right direction to find the treasure.

Chapter 8

Define and Direct

"Some have dreams, but have goals. Life goals. Monthly goals. Yearly goals. Daily goals. I try to give myself a goal every day." "Have goals. And understand that, to achieve these goals, you must apply discipline and consistency...not just on Tuesday and then miss a few days." "Continue to strive. Continue to have goals. Continue to progress."

-Denzel Washington

If you have ever shot a gun, a bow, or golfed you understand this concept. When you shoot a gun, you place your crosshairs on the target you want to hit. Your goal should be to watch the bullet hit the target through the scope. If you remove your eye from the scope, or flinch your body, you will not be accurate. The same goes for archery. When you are shooting a compound bow, you must keep your pin on the target and have a smooth release. If your eye comes off the target at any point, you are going to miss the intended target.

For those that golf, you also have a target. That is the hole. You look at the hole and study it. You come up with a game plan for how you will play your ball to get to the hole in as few hits as possible. You have to determine how you play the "dogleg". Are you laying up to the water or trying to clear it? If there is a bunker, how will you avoid it? You have obstacles in your way, and it is your job to make a plan to get around them or go through them. If you play golf like me, the hole will not go as planned, and as a result, you will have to pivot to make the best of the situation.

These situations are analogous to your life. You must DEFINE the targets in your life and DIRECT a plan for getting there. Everything looks great on paper, but just like golf, your plan will have obstacles. When you encounter those obstacles, you have to keep your eye on the target and keep moving forward.

When you define a target or a want, everything else becomes simple. Picture this: you are standing at a starting line and you are in a lane. Down your lane is the target that you have set your site on. If you step into another lane or take your eye off the target, it is going to take you longer to reach your target. If you continue to detour out of your lane with distractions and excuses, you may never make it to your target. The more you focus on the target, the quicker the path to get there will be.

Here's the problem: MOST PEOPLE DO NOT DEFINE THE TARGET.

As a result, they go straight, hang a left, then a right, then back track, then move forward, then left, then straight, then right, until they feel lost and "stuck". Each one of those detours on your journey was a distraction from your target. You must DEFINE what your target is, and you must focus your undivided attention on it. Distractions and excuses have to be eliminated.

If you are living a life where you feel lost and unfulfilled, it is most likely because you have not set any targets for yourself. Stop going through the motions because "it is what it is." Instead, every single thing you do should be intentional toward your identified targets and the life you want to live. People who DEFINE their targets and IN-TENTIONALLY DIRECT their attention towards those targets are fulfilled and driven.

When it comes to goals and dreams, timelines should be considered, but they are not always necessary[2]. The reality is, you don't know how long it is going to take. All you know is that you have to keep moving toward the target. If you create an imaginary timeline and you do not make it, most people will quit because they have failed to achieve their goal in the arbitrary time they created. It may take you longer than you think to hit your intended target, or it might happen sooner than you had planned. Regardless, you must stay *directed* because problems will arise, and you will have to create a solution.

As you move toward your target, distractions are going to jump out of every corner. Excuses are going to pop up in your mind daily. Your stress and anxiety will grow. So, when you start to succumb to the distractions and excuses, ask yourself: "Does this get me to my target?" If the answer is NO, then ask yourself: "Why am I doing this?" IF the answer is YES, carry on. Do not overthink. There is no maybe, or kinda, or it might, or it could; it has to be a definitive YES or NO.

---

2 *Timelines can be helpful once you start to figure out a process. It is unrealistic and unhealthy to give yourself a week to lose 50 pounds. With that being said, after you lose X amount of weight, have a solid and healthy plan, then you can create a REALISTIC timeline to lose 10 pounds.*

Targets should be clear and simple, but most people make them difficult.

A simple example is weight loss:

- Target weight: 185 pounds (DEFINE)
- Where do I have to DIRECT my attention?
- Eat Clean- (This might look different for everyone)
- Workout for 1 hour each day
- Eliminate alcohol
- Do this until I reach 185....simple.

Example of Business Revenue:

- 1,000,000.00 in sales (DEFINE)
- Where do I have to DIRECT my attention?
- My product cost $1,000.00 – I need 1,000 buyers
- My conversion rate is 50%- I need to contact 2,000 people
- 2000/365 = I need to contact AT least 5.5 people per day for a year.
- DIRECT your attention to contacting 5.5 people per day.
- In a year, you should be close to $1,000,000.00 in sales.

It really is that simple. When you intentionally focus on something, that is what will grow. If you let the distractions and excuses get in the way of your targets, then expect to be stuck in the same place you currently are, or the path to your targets will take twice as long.

Your targets should be **specific.** "I want to lose weight" is not a specific target. "I want to make money" is not a specific target. Set specific targets of what you want to achieve and create an intentional plan to get there. There are 100 different ways to build targets. Some people like daily targets. Some people have weekly targets. Some people have 30 or 90 day targets. Others have one target for the entire year. I am not going to tell you how to structure your targets. You have to determine that yourself.

Refer to the business example above:

- Example of a daily target: Contact 5.5 people
- Example of a weekly target: Generate 20k in revenue

- Example of 60 day Target: In 60 days, generate 240,000 and make 70 contacts.

It is up to you to decide what targets you want for each part of your life and how you will structure them. I like to make a bigger target and then create a process to get there. Let's go back to the example of making $1,000,000.00 in sales: I would create a daily target of reaching six people per day and closing half or more of them. Understand that some days, you might go 0/6 and other days you might go 6/6. Whatever you do, do NOT stop contacting six people per day. Keep moving toward the target.

Ultimately, Your life is up to you. You have to decide what you want to focus your attention on each day. WHAT YOU FOCUS ON GROWS. If you direct your attention to drama, gossip, and parties, those things will grow. If you focus on a personal skill set, it will grow. Focus on the negative, you will have more negativity. This is the Law of Attraction: what you put out into the universe will be returned.

Chapter 9

Four Cornerstones

Cornerstone (n): 1. an important quality or feature on which a particular thing depends or is based. 2. a stone that forms the base of a corner of a building, joining two walls

Most structures have a minimum of four corners because it makes them structurally sound. Once you have a solid foundation, you can build on top of it. The same for anything you do. You must first master the basics and fundamentals. Too many people try to build without first setting the foundation. Creating a solid foundation gives you the ability to keep building. When something happens that brings your house down, you can build it back up even quicker because you have the foundations and lessons to fall back on.

It is important to establish a foundation and use it to build the rest of your life. The 4 cornerstones[3] that I use are:

- **Character-** Ourselves, being selfish. Selfishness leads to selflessness.

- **Connection-** Forming strong relationships.

- **Creation-** Facilitates growth and progress.

- **Continuance-** Our results. Understanding why we are where we are.

By focusing on these, I built a better ME. I built better relationships. I got rid of the relationships that hindered me. I built a better business. Now, I understand my results and can adjust when they are not the results I want.

I keep them in this order intentionally. YOU should always come first. This might seem selfish. It is. If we cannot take care of ourselves,

---

3 *This is not a newfound idea that I have created. These methods have been used for years. It is simply using word recognition to help you create an understanding and also help you to remember the meaning or cause. You have been using this method since kindergarten to learn your ABCs and 123s. It simply reminds your brain when you begin to question the choices you are making. It also categorizes each part of your life. I chose these four cornerstones because they have helped me tremendously in my journey.*

how can we take care of others? If I am broke, how can I give back to those in need? If I am fat, how can I teach the generation behind me to be healthy? If my relationships are a mess, how can I teach my kids the value of good relationships? Simply put, you cannot help others until you help yourself.

Character - This is YOU!

The old cliché reads: character is how you act when nobody is looking. This is partly true, but character really is making the best decisions for yourself and your personal environment at all times.

If you see a piece of trash on the ground, no matter where you are, pick it up and throw it away. Wipe your piss off the seat. Leave things better than you found them. Take care of your body, mind, and spirit.

How do you feel about yourself? If your kids described your character, what would they say? If you don't have kids and you are young, what would your friends say or your teachers say? Are you a hard worker? Are you kind? Do you care about what you put into your mouth? Do you care about what you consume with your eyes and ears?

Most of us try to dictate our character by what others would say about us, but we have to consider how we feel about ourselves, first. That is the ultimate flex. Can you go to bed at night feeling like you did everything in your power to better yourself? Can you say you gave the day 110%? Did you go ALL IN on whatever you were doing? When you lay your head on your pillow, you should be able to cozily sleep because YOU WON THE DAY.

Like many, I was involved in high school sports. I was never the most talented or the most athletic. Yet, the one thing I had over everyone I ever played against was my ability to compete and outwork my opponents. That was the cheat code to my athletic career - OUTWORK EVERYONE.

I HATE to lose, but if you do beat me, chances are you are better and more skilled than me. I never cried after losing a game. Why? Because I knew what I brought to the table. I knew I left it all on the floor or the field and controlled only what I could. Sometimes you still lose. But you must learn and move on. If you're not giving everything you have every game, that is when you *should* cry yourself to sleep.

It is the same in the game of life. When you half ass everything you do, chances are you are going to be a miserable person who points the finger and whines about their circumstances. Just like hard work, your character is something *you can control.* You can control your emotions, your fitness, your nutrition, your reading, your television, and your conversations. So, when you go to bed at night, it is all on YOU as you reflect on your day.

Spiritually, you have to find peace in your life. I choose God. I pray and talk with God each morning. I will not tell you what to believe , but believe in something. Spend time alone and meditate. Clear your mind. Breathe and give your mind and body some relief if only for a few minutes. From the moment we wake up, our mind is racing 800 miles per hour, so do yourself a favor and slow it down and shut it off at some point.

In the end, you must create the human you were meant to be. Looking good and being your best creates a confidence that will carry you through almost any hard time. Once you get yourself in order, the entire game of life changes. It gets more manageable and more fun because you are WINNING every single day.

Connection - AKA
"Relationship Capital"

Who or what are you connected with in your life? What types of people do you have around you? When you spend time with friends, what do you spend your time talking about? Politics? Weather? Problems? Or do you spend your time talking about growth and building? This has a lot to do with where the trajectory of your life is headed or where the trajectory of your business is headed. If you are not connecting with people who push you to grow and improve, you are doing yourself a disservice. After spending time with your friends, do you feel an excitement and a drive to push forward to excel in your life, business, and career? Or do you feel angry and dragged down?

If you are connected and surrounded by negative people, then you are going to develop a negative mindset. Now, there is power in negative thinking when used correctly. Unfortunately, most people do not use negative thinking as a tool, but rather a crutch as to why they cannot do something. We can turn negativity into a weapon for success. For example, when you throw out an idea and someone immediately tells you that you cannot do it, this might fuel you to prove them wrong. In this instance, you have turned that negative mindset into fuel for excelling in life. You want people in your life that are going to say, "Hell yeah, you should 100% do that. Let me know how I can help." You also want them to challenge you and speak truth to you.

It is also important that we have people in our lives who support our visions no matter how whacky they might seem. There is an old saying that reads: "You are the average of the 5 people you spend the most time with." If you spend your time around people who are stuck in life and really have no vision, you will end up the average of that. On the flip side, if you spend time with people who are driven and are growing and expanding their lives, you will see your growth expedited. How many millionaires do you see hanging out with "thousandaires"? Very few. And if they are, they are most likely speaking, mentoring, and or teaching those who have not reached that level.

This is why I am so adamant that you get the right people around you. If people are not adding value to you, they need to be cut out of your life. If people are not honest with you, cut the cord. If people fake-support you, they need to go.I am not saying you have to cut them out completely, but you should not be spending the majority of your time with them, you should be mindful of who you are taking advice from. After all, you wouldn't take nutrition and fitness advice from a fat trainer would you?

Connection is the key to any successful business,organization, or marriage. To be successful in business relationships are number one. Relationships create abundance. You must understand and value your relationships with your customers, employees, investors, and business mentors. The more people you know, the more likely they are going to buy from you.

How do you get around more of the right people? Build your own table. I formed a group of business owners that came together and met once every two weeks. We sipped whiskey and talked business. We helped each other learn and grow. I still have a relationship with each one of those owners, and we still do business together. I took successful business owners that I know out to lunch and they talked about themselves and the growth of their companies. I spent most of my time listening and asking questions.

Now, they also have become customers. People create a relationship with your company, and if you are taking care of them and fostering that relationship, you will continue to win over and over and over again.

Lastly, if you are not connecting with your spouse on a regular basis, chances are your marriage is going to suffer. My wife and I establish one night a week for date night. We go out on a date. Usually, it is nothing special. We go have ice cream or coffee. Sometimes, we go for a walk. Whatever it is, the intention is to spend time together and talk. We talk about all sorts of things - life, business, kids, etc. Our conversations usually revolve around growth and the future. We do not go out to gossip and speak ill of others. The point is, we are connecting with each other consistently and intentionally.

Creation

What are you creating each day, week, month, or year? What are you creating in your life that is helping you grow and achieve at a high level? What systems have you created in your life and business to keep things moving orderly and efficiently? Do you have targets? Do you have goals? What do you do to create discipline to achieve those goals?

Creation is key to overcoming major obstacles in your life. Many people encounter a problem and never solve it. Their small problems build up over time because they never created a way to handle them. This might be a small disagreement you are having with your spouse and a solution is never created.

Ben Franklin once said, "A small hole can sink a great ship." If we let the small problems stack up, they will sink us into darkness, depression, anxiety, and broken relationships. How do we solve those problems in our lives? Most people will put a band-aid on it or "brush it under the rug." We tend to do this with our personal obstacles. We keep looking past them or avoid them. But, as we avoid them, they build up and eat at us from the inside. We might appear fine on the outside to others, but internally we are a sinking ship.

I created and tested many avenues to help me overcome these issues, but the one I found the most beneficial was creating a routine that FITS ME. At the writing of this book, I have done 905 days in a row of my routine. My mornings look like this:

1. I wake up around 4:00 am and show gratitude. "Thank you for another day."

2. I read and study a book based around self-development and/ or business.

3. I read and study one page of the bible.

4. I journal until I am done. I do not have a word requirement or time limit.[4]

5. I talk with God- I pray and I listen.

I tested many different things before I came to the conclusion that this was best for me. This is not a one size fits all approach. You have to CREATE and TEST. Create a routine, try it for a month, and if you are not feeling any different, then move on and test again. It might take months to figure out what fits you and what helps you, but do not give up on it. I tried cold showers, saunas, walks outside, meditation, breath work, stretching, etc. This routine is what has fit me the best at this point in my life. It will eventually change and evolve into something different. Your routine will most likely be forever evolving and it should be because as you grow, things around you change.

In your business, what are you creating to keep it moving efficiently? Have you created a marketing plan? Have you created systems for workflow? Do you have open lines of communication? Even if you are a one man show, eventually you will grow into a two man show, then a four man show, etc. Start building the systems now while you are alone, so you can be prepared when you start to hire people. Systems create continuity and slim down wasted time trying to "figure things out". It creates a stream of communication for you and your team.

If you are not creating new goals and targets regularly, do not expect to grow and expand. If you own a business, you should have targets you are trying to hit. These are not always financial targets, but all the underlying details that result in financial growth. That could be contacting five to ten potential customers on a daily basis. Creating daily wins will take care of the overall big picture, but you must deliberately create those systems and habits that help you get to your daily wins. Everyone wants to go for the home run, but the reality in life and

---

4 *I do not just journal to journal. I reflect. I ask myself why. I work through my triggers and my emotions. I use it to study myself and be real about who I am and what it is I am working through. It is no bullshit. Many of my entries are dark, but it is the reality of me working through my troubles. I find solutions to problems. Many of you can do this in your head. It works best for me to write it out. If you are struggling to find peace or understand, I would suggest you start this practice.*

business is that you have to hit a bunch of singles and doubles consistently. Create a way to get these small wins each day, each week, each month, and watch the big goals take care of themselves.

What you create is not always going to work, so instead of whining about it and giving up, you have to pivot and adjust. Things rarely go as planned. You have to have the adaptability to adjust your creations to achieve the results you are looking for.

Continuance

This is the most humbling of all the cornerstones. Continuance is the reflection of your results.

- Have you lost the weight?

- Have you made the money?

- Have you built the connections?

- Are your creations working for you?

- Are you growing or are you stagnant?

RESULTS DO NOT LIE! You are either WINNING or you are LOSING. Now is when you look back at your progress and be honest with yourself. Being honest with yourself is one of the hardest things we do. The person you lie to the most is yourself, but it is very simple to call bullshit on yourself because the results are in front of your face. Sometimes it hurts.

If you are not where you set your targets, what needs to change? What did you do that took you off course? What excuses did you make that kept you from hitting your targets? Did you really call five extra people five days a week or did you take days off sporadically?

Most people cannot follow through with what they say they are going to do for an extended period of time. When we start something, it is new and exciting and then it gets monotonous and boring. We begin to despise it and then stop doing what we need to do to make it work. Then we blame the economy, employees, vendors, etc., but the REAL REAL truth is YOU ARE NOT HOLDING YOURSELF ACCOUNT-ABLE. You are letting yourself slip through the cracks. You are letting outside forces control your time. When your time is controlled, your life is controlled. You have to figure out the common denominator for your problems. 9 out of 10 times that common denominator *is you.*

When you reflect on your results and you do not like them, you need to figure out why the results are what they are. You need to determine where you are slipping. You need to determine the changes you need to make. It is not your trainer, nutritionist, business coach, friends, family, kids, economy, or any other factor. It is YOU. The minute you recognize that YOU are responsible for your results is when your results will start to change. You have to understand the results and understand why they are what they are. Then take ACTION in correcting the behaviors that have given you the results that you have.

Chapter 10

Be Intentional

Intentional (adj.) - Done on purpose. Deliberate

When we decide we want a change in our lives, we tend to put "the pedal to the metal" and try to get it done all at once. In my experience, this has never worked. You cannot fix everything all at once, and it will not happen overnight. You have to be intentional to create change.

Take a moment and think about your daily activities. Is each day filled with chaos and stress? Do you always feel like you never have enough time to get everything done? Are you distracted by your phone, email, pointless conversations, and social media?

Chaos and stress are created. These two things do not manifest out of thin air. I do not believe we were meant to live a life of angst from the moment we wake up to the moment we go to bed. I believe the chaos and stress we feel is self-inflicted most of the time. Of course, things happen that are out of our control, but we also can choose how we receive it and how we react to it. We also have the choice to stop it.

Most of the chaos and stress in your life is dictated by how intentional you are with your daily habits. How intentional are you with your time, your words, your work, and your reactions?

Do you find it odd that many people can get 10x the work done in a day than others? It is not rocket science. It is the art of intention and being intentional with your time. If you are in the middle of answering emails and you are distracted by a text message, which then leads to being distracted by social media, which then leads to sharing the memes and reels, and then you try to get back to the email you were working on, it is going to cause stress and chaos.

Being intentional is being present in the moment of writing that email and cutting off all distractions. The simple email you were writing may have taken five minutes of your time, but due to your lack of intention it has now become a 30 minute ordeal. That is 25 minutes of distractions and wasted time from what you needed to accomplish. Here comes the feeling of STRESS AND CHAOS. Now you are in a rush to get it done and you feel behind with what you need to accomplish. The stress ball is now rolling downhill and collecting more stress as it goes.

The world is more distracting than ever. Social media, kids, news, emails, texts, phone calls, family. . .the list goes on. We have devices now that make us accessible 24/7 to anyone in the world. The cool thing about these devices is that they have an "OFF" button, or a "Do Not Disturb" feature. You just have to be INTENTIONAL and use it.

Being intentional is no mistake and it is not easy. It is very uncomfortable and inconvenient, but it is the secret to creating a successful life.

Be INTENTIONAL with your time. If you live in a world of chaos and stress, it is time to think about how you are spending your day.

Be INTENTIONAL with your money. A common theme: make more, spend more. You will never get ahead. You need to be intentional with where your money goes. Investments, kids, cost of living, saving etc., should all be intentional.

Be INTENTIONAL with your relationships. Relationship capital is the biggest driver in business and life. Without those connections, your business and life will struggle. How are your relationships with others? How do you treat your coworkers? How do you treat your friends? Are you upgrading your relationships? Your relationships will dictate your future growth or stagnation.

Be INTENTIONAL with your health. Health is no mistake. Exercise and eat healthy. Both are very simple tasks, but must be done with intention.

Be INTENTIONAL with you kids. Do you spend time with your children one on one? Do you make family dinners intentional? Do you intentionally instill positive principles into your children? Remember: Kids are a product of their environment.

Be INTENTIONAL with your spouse. Why do 50% of marriages fail? Marriage is intentional and you must work on it intentionally. Transparency, weekly date nights, intimacy, money, kids, etc - prioritize your spouse.

If you want your life to be different you have to be INTENTIONAL. Discipline is hard. Saying no is hard, but the more you do ANY-

THING the easier it becomes. Once you have defined what it is you want in your life, you have to INTENTIONALLY direct your attention to it. Wealth, six packs, and purposeful lives were not built by accident. They were built with Intentional acts completed over an extended period of time.

YOU are capable of living a life of PURPOSE if YOU are INTENTIONAL and DIRECTED. DEFINE AND DIRECT.

About the Author

Nick was born and raised in central Wyoming. He spent most of his time growing up competing in sports, hunting, fishing, and spending time outdoors. After high school, he went to the University of Wyoming and managed a .6 GPA the first semester. He dropped out of college. He worked various jobs including night shift work and roofing. While roofing, he was asked to assist coaching 9th grade football. Coaching became a passion and he went back to school to become a teacher. Based on his previous academic success, just to obtain the required GPA to become a teacher, he had to pull a 4.0 for multiple semesters. He is terrible at school, so this was difficult for him and he worked very hard to achieve it.

Nick worked as an English teacher (Do NOT judge the grammar or mechanics of this book - he never said he was good at it) and coached all 8-12 in football and basketball. While teaching he received a masters degree in Organizational Management from Chadron State. He graduated from that program with a 3.8 GPA. After teaching for about 8 years, Nick quit to pursue his business "side hustles" in landscaping and sign manufacturing. Eventually, he sold the landscape company for a small amount, but he has built his sign company into a seven -figure business. As of today, he still owns and operates Western Sign and Design, which has grown into a 7-figure company. However, he had 5 other companies that he tried to get off the ground that failed miserably.

Nick has been blessed with two imperfect kids that he loves dearly. He spends a lot of our summers and weekends watching them compete in sports and activities. He has been married to his wife for 15 years and she has been instrumental in the growth of their business and lives. They continue to grow and evolve each day.

He is still passionate about coaching and leading people. Nick truly wants people to succeed and live fulfilled lives. He has not lived a perfect or direct life for his whole life, but over the past 5-6 years, he has changed his focus to creating a better version of himself, and it has impacted everything around him in a positive way. He wants to share that with people in hopes that they will experience it as well.